ONE HUNDRED AND FIFTY-TWO DAYS

One Hundred and Fifty-Two Days

Giles Paley-Phillips

unbound

First published in 2020

Unbound

6th Floor Mutual House, 70 Conduit Street, London W1S 2GF

www.unbound.com

Text design by Patty Rennie

A CIP record for this book is available from the British Library

ISBN 978-1-78352-770-0 (hardback)
ISBN 978-1-78352-773-1 (ebook)

Printed in Great Britain by
CPI Group (UK) Ltd, Croydon CR0 4YY

1 3 5 7 9 8 6 4 2

To absent friends, Brenda Paley-Phillips,
Charles Paley-Phillips, Sarah Race,
Bill and Queenie Carpenter

Grief is a lonely journey that many
people may try to join you on, to listen
and comfort, but the journey is yours
alone; just don't try and go too fast.

To live in hearts we leave behind is not to die.

Thomas Campbell, Poet (1777–1844)

The Change

Physio Day 108

The clapping under my arms,
my back,
    my chest
        is relentless.
'The infection was really severe,' she says.
'From your notes it appears
you've been coming here for quite a while.'
The clapping is percussive, and I close my eyes.
The rhythm is somehow soothing, then I ready myself.
They say the position is crucial to make the procedure effective,
to loosen the secretions caused by the infection.
'That's it,' she says,
'you're doing a good job.'
Clap… Cough…
and the cup below becomes stained with spit;
each cough removes just a little bit more.
It's been weeks since I started.
I hope it's nearly all gone.

Before

I try to remember
what it felt like before.
I try to remember
before it all happened,
before she was ill,
before I was ill.
I try to remember...
before.

The new physio Day 108

The physio is new.
Her name is Freya;
   she's from Australia.
I've never met anyone from Australia before.
She likes to talk
   but I find it hard to listen;
      too many thoughts
in my head... blocking my ears.
I wish I could
just listen
but my mind is on
other things.

Freya

Freya is tall, maybe six feet,
or maybe not quite, but tall.
And slender and beautiful and her hair is bright blue, like sapphire,
and short and sharp. And she has a tattoo
on her wrist of a small black bird
flying, then another beginning to soar
up her arm.
And she has a confidence I've
never experienced before, and a gentleness –
she seems genuine
and real.
And I'm hooked.

Soon

Dad is in the waiting room.
He sits very still, staring at the space
between himself and the door.

I try to bring him round.
'How's Mum?' I ask.
      'The same,' he says.
It was a silly question really.
'I wish I could see her,' I say.
'You will soon,' he says.
'As soon as you are better,
as soon as your chest has cleared.
She's just too weak right now.
Soon… I promise.'

Looking down

Looking down at my feet,
I feel my face go red.
I feel heat in my cheeks,
Looking down at my feet.
And the heat
in my cheeks,
it almost hurts.
I feel
angry.
I feel disappointed.

Run

As we walk towards the entrance,
I feel like running,
running through the doors. Every
fibre in my body twitches, every
nerve, to run
and run
and run.
But I don't.

There are always things

There are always things we don't want.
Always things we don't want to happen
to ourselves.
We want it to be happening
to other people,
                    not ourselves.
There are often things we can't accept,
things we can't believe are true.
Things we have to accept;
but we can't,
even though we have to.

Can't get to sleep Day 108

Can't get to sleep.
My chest feels tight,
like a heavy weight is lying
on top of me. I take deep
breaths, each followed by
a cough.
A splutter.
A wince.
Every time I look at the clock
another hour goes past, and
I want to sleep so badly,
but my chest
and my brain won't let me.
Thoughts, just bubbling around.
Why can't I see her?
I'm feeling better now.
A cough.
A splutter.
A wince.
I can go back to school,
but I am not well enough
to see her, not yet.
But soon.
A cough.
A splutter.
A wince.

Saying goodbye

Today I said goodbye to Mum.
It's starting to get cold outside,
winter coming around again.
It's 1991. I'm hoping 1992
will be better.
She is going in,
just for a little while.
More treatments.
We carry on like normal.
She's sat on the sofa, dressing gown on,
the sun burning a glow on the side
of her face, through the curtain.
Nana Q was going to walk with me,
walk with me to school,
even though I'm old enough.
I usually walk on my own, but today
they thought Nana Q should go
with me.
'It's time you got going,' Mum says,
and as I lean down to her, she
pulls me in and I feel her shaking.
Uncontrollable shaking. Her grip
is weak, and she whispers
in my ear and I can't make it out
and I ask her to repeat, but she can't
hold back her tears, and as I pull
away, I wish I'd asked again.

Be good, pet

Nana Q and I walk to school,
neither of us saying anything
until we reach the front entrance
and Nana Q says,
'Be good, pet,'
and wanders away.
I look at the entrance,
but I want to walk away,
and not go inside.
I look at the entrance,
and I feel my heart speed up.
I feel my chest tighten
and I just want to walk away,
but I don't.
I just walk straight ahead,
and in the classroom
Luka tries to throw his bag onto the desk
and it smashes straight through the window.
Everyone is laughing
and Luka is running out
to get his bag
just as Mr Moore
enters the room.
Dan and I look at each other
and we can't stop laughing.
Maybe today won't be so bad.

Green, yellow and brown nuggets

It started off as a cold,
then a sore throat, then I had
a high temperature, a fever, exhaustion.
Just like Mum.
But mine was a chest infection,
bacteria affecting my alveoli.
Then came the phlegm, the chest pain,
the tightness, the time off school, the loss
of appetite. Pneumonia, the doctor said,
and I'm going to need help to
release the rest of the phlegm,
the green, yellow and brown nuggets,
the things that keep me awake at night.
I won't have to stay in hospital –
I can get better at home,
but I'll need help, so the
doctor gives me tablets, antibiotics,
and refers me to a physiotherapist.
And I haven't been able to see Mum, not
while I'm poorly,
not while I've got this phlegm.
Not for weeks.

Why this?

Why this?
Why now?
Why me?

Will I ever know?

Excuses Day 54

Dad left the house
before I woke up.
Nana Q made excuses
about him meeting up
with someone.
Nana Q is always making excuses.
Always letting him off.
He is her son.
I wonder if he would do the same
for me.

Every morning is the same...

Every morning is the same:
I get up and come out of my bedroom
to be faced by silence,
before I hear,
      'Get ready for school,' shouted from the kitchen,
as the sound of a plate
smashing on the floor
fills the air.
It's hard for my Nana Q,
doing this alone.

Morning taste

I go to brush my teeth
but there is no toothpaste,
so I just use water, and it's cold,
but the morning taste is still
in my mouth
and I feel scummy.

A stranger

I often wander
  around our house...
feeling like
a stranger.
Like I'm in someone else's house.
Everything looks different.
Everything feels different.
Will today be the day?
Will today be the day
I'm recognised?

I used to

I used to enjoy school, but now
I dread it.
I used to enjoy seeing people, but now
I just want to be on my own.
Quiet…
unnoticed
a nobody
a no one.
I used to enjoy
mucking about,
being silly, tormenting the caretaker,
getting him annoyed, moving stuff around
in the classrooms.
We all did it –
the entire class.
But then it changed,
everything changed:
my mum's life, my dad's life,
my life changed.
The moment they said
she had to stay in
was the same time
I no longer wanted
to join in.

I am lanky

I am fourteen, nearly fifteen.
I am tall for my age…
The others in my class
call me 'lanky'.
I don't mind…
They could easily mention
that my clothes appear unwashed,
that my clothes smell stale.
      That I smell stale.
But they don't.

A day is a day is a day Day 101

A day is a day is a day.
Each rolls into the next.
The frosty tarmac
of the school playground
glistens under the sun
and I can see my breath
                float out into the air.
A day is a day is a day.
Each rolls into the next.
The same sounds,
the same blank expressions
staring back at me.
A day is a day is
a
day.

I pretend

I head straight to the classroom
where Dan is sat, in the place
next to my place.
He greets me with a nod
and continues to read his
magazine about American wrestling.
Everyone always says to Dan that
American wrestling isn't real, that
they fake it, that
they choreograph the fights, that
the wrestlers are more like dancers
than fighters. Dan doesn't like this,
so I pretend,
I pretend to believe it too.
I pretend so that Dan will be my friend…
my ally.
I pretend so that I have someone
who believes me too.
I pretend because…

                        I'm good at

pretending.

Breaks

Breaks used to be fun.
Dan, Luka, Nazim and I
playing football, and commentating,
commentating
like it's *Match of the Day*.
'Nazim picks up the ball on the halfway line
and spreads it wide to Luka Stevens on the left.'
And I wait in the goal,
waiting for them to shoot,
waiting to make a save,
to claim the glory.
'It's Rogers, Dan Rogers with the shot,
the shot for United, but it's saved,
saved by the Palace goalkeeper.
What a brilliant save!'
Now I just commentate
in my head as the others play.
Commentating in my head
like it's *Match of the Day*.

The flat

We've just moved.
We're in a flat now. They'd planned it
before she went to hospital.
It is easier to manage
for Dad.
There are two rooms: one for me,
one for Dad.
Nana Q moved in too.
Nana Q sleeps on the sofa in the lounge,
next to the little white kitchen.
The walls in my room have mould
in the corners. On the ceiling. Round the window.
Dad says it's the condensation…
vapour cooling, turning to water, rotting the walls.
The ceiling. Round the windows. The room.
The flat,
      all rotting.
Like Mum.

Nana Q   Day 15

Each morning I find
Nana Q asleep on the sofa.
Mouth wide open, body motionless.
I wonder if this is what a dead person looks like.
At night
            she likes to arrange the things in her bag.
Her betting slips,
her football pools,
her lottery tickets,
her loose change,
her notes,
her lists...
            her endless lists,
the contents of which we never quite know...
Maybe...
it's the chores she will never do.
Maybe...
it's the things she will never buy.
That is how she spends her nights.
      Arranging.
This is how she spends her mornings... sleeping.
Snoring
and muttering
about horses, dogs, bets,
over and over again.

Little triumph   Day 116

It is the new physio again.
She speaks between back claps.
I didn't notice before
that she
speaks in rhythms.
I remember her name –
it's Freya.
      Clap…
'Did you have a good week?'
      Clap…
'What are you doing at the weekend?'
          Clap…
                Clap…
And I excrete another little gift into her cup.
She says,
'Good one, mate, that's a proper big one!'
She is genuinely excited by my little triumph.
'You should keep that one and frame it.'
I really like her.

Secretions

'The main function,' she says,
'is the removal of tracheobronchial secretions.
The removal of airway obstruction.
The reduction of airway resistance.
To help your lungs recover.'
'To help you recover,' she says.
'To help,' she says.
'To help you,' she says.
'You,' she says.
'Recover,' she says.
Recover.

Not an anything

I wonder how to talk to her.
I wonder if she would be
interested in the things
I might have to say. I wonder
if she would relate to me.
Then I tell myself
not to be so stupid.
Someone like her would never
want to know about
someone like me, not really,
not beyond this moment,
this appointment and the next.
I'm just a patient
with a need…
                              for help.
Not a friend, not a love interest,
not an anything.
I've always been nervous
around girls.
Girls like Daisy,
like Jade, the popular girls.
I'm never sure what to say,
how to be me,
how to actually show me
as I really am.
I've never felt a kiss
from a girl
or even been held

at the school disco.
I just watched
as my friends kissed girls.
Some played a game
of passing a Polo between their mouths,
but I never got to play.
I just watched.

Weekend

I'm supposed to go swimming
with Dan, with Nazim, with Luka… my friends.
I don't see them much.
I'd like to see them.
But I've got to go to Nana Q's flat.
Nana Q needs some more clothes, and she wants her trolley.
She calls it her 'bogie'.
I ask her why, but she doesn't have an answer.
    Nan never has an answer.
        She just creates lots of questions.

Swimming

Before all this, before
Mum was ill, before I was ill,
I used to hang out with my friends
at the sports centre
on Saturday mornings.
We'd go swimming.
At the fun splash
hour, we'd dive-bomb each other
and take the piss out of the lifeguards,
who'd get cross
with us…
The pool was always really warm
and the scent of chlorine was strong.
We used to say
the stronger the smell, the more people
had urinated in the pool. We'd accuse each other
of doing it, being the biggest pisser in the pool.
Saturday mornings at the sports centre, in that pool,
we regressed to silly games and taunts,
but we loved it, I loved it,
but it seems like another
person's life right now.

My history of swimming

What feels like a lifetime ago,
Mum would drive me
and Nana Q
to the beach on the hottest days
during the summer holidays.
Dad would be working.
She'd pack the car with bodyboards,
floats, and buckets to collect stones.
I'd thrash around in the sea,
my mum supporting the sides
of the bodyboard.
We'd laugh each time
I slipped off. I felt safe.
I felt comforted
every time she'd
scoop me up, her arms
protecting me
like a blanket.

Just behind

Nana Q strides in front.
I trail just behind… downwind.
Nana Q greets everyone she meets
with an 'Are ya keepin' canny, like?'
I trail just behind…
Nana Q floats through the town
in and out of shops
filling up her bogie
with this and that,
nothing I can identify clearly
or can be bothered to.
Nana Q heads to the betting shop.
I trail just behind…

Terminal orchid

I can see curtains ruffling, like bird feathers, in the downstairs
windows.
As we approach the entrance,
a frail-looking lady,
                a neighbour,
appears from nowhere.
She says she's been keeping an eye on Nana Q's place.
Nana Q smiles…
                then mouths, 'Nosy old bitch!' to me
when her back has turned.
I help Nana Q up the stairs… to her flat.
Flat number 5.
The number on the door is falling off
and the orchid plant outside, to the left,
   is dying.
Nana Q says it's terminal
then lets out a really loud burp.
She never ceases to surprise me.

Inside

As Nana Q opens the door,
we are greeted with a waft of stale air.
Nana Q breathes it in;
    she loves this flat.
A cluttered hallway leads us to the lounge
where she keeps her hoards.
   Her newspapers,
     her magazines,
        her letters… her photos… her bills.
Her words.
Her words and text.
Her words and text and pictures.
This is how she remembers things.
Her lists.
    Her life.

Tea

Nana Q painstakingly makes tea
for us.
For her.
She pre-heats the cup
and fills the kettle just enough
for two cups of tea.
I say I don't want a cup of tea.
But Nana Q is concentrating.
She waits by the kettle,
waiting for it to reach boiling point.
Nana Q insists the water must boil
for perfect tea.
I've never understood
the way she does things
as her tea always tastes bad.
She pours two cups
and I say I don't want a cup of tea.
'Drink up!' she says.
My mum is really ill,
my dad is never here, and
I don't want a cup of tea.

A mum with hair and a dad with a smile

There is a picture
by Nana Q's TV,
just to the left,
next to an empty vase.
It's all of us:
Mum, Dad, Nana Q and me.
We're in a restaurant,
a Chinese restaurant.
We're celebrating
a birthday.
My birthday.
Mum still has hair, and Dad
is smiling. I remember
laughing,
laughing so hard,
laughing at Nana Q spitting food,
spitting out the food she was
enjoying, green food.
Dad had told her it was seaweed, and
that was it, straight out of her mouth,
back on the plate, a gesture
of contempt, disgust, like
we'd played a trick on her, but
then she laughed
and I laughed
and Dad laughed
and Mum laughed.
A mum with hair and
a dad with a smile.

Back home

We're back home.
Dad isn't here.
The house is cold.
Nana Q tells me it is the coldest winter for twenty years.
Nana Q always talks about the weather.
I think it's what old people do,
just talk about the weather,
 and their aches and pains.
I wipe my finger along the windowsill.
It's wet;
 the condensation has caused a pool of water.
Cold and wet... my fingers now pressed against
the glass,
waiting for Dad.
Always waiting.
With the lights on.

Like being alone

I often feel alone
without actually being alone.
Alone with my mind,
alone with my thoughts,
and they attack me
like a disease attacks,
like the disease attacking Mum.
But I'm never alone,
                              not really.
And sometimes all I really want
is to be alone,
      fully alone,
so I don't have to live
with the constant thoughts.

Dinner

Nana Q cooks dinner.
Nana Q always cooks dinner now.
Nana Q invites Jean from next door to join us.
Jean is older than Nana Q
    and she has a walking stick,
        which she wields like a baseball bat.
Tonight, we are having boiled ham,
pease pudding and boiled potatoes.
Everything on the plate looks grey,
like the food has been stripped of colour
    … of taste.
'Eat up!' Nana Q says.
I look at Jean.
She smiles; bits of meat are stuck between her teeth.
'Lovely, isn't it?' she says.
I look back at my plate
and wonder when Dad will be home.

Midnight

I hear the front door rattling downstairs,
   then the sound of keys dropping on the ground outside.
I throw my duvet off
      and I switch on the lamp beside my bed.
I ignore the clock as I edge to the door.
Dad sits at the bottom of the stairs,
   attempting to remove his shoes.
He looks like a child,
        … pulling at the laces
… tugging at the heels.
His head starts to bob up and down,
and I can't tell
if he is laughing…
or crying.
I turn and head back to my room.
I pass the clock;
     this time I look.
It reads midnight.

In and out

My brain won't switch off
and I go in and out
of sleep.
I tried to listen,
but I can't hear anything from Dad's room.
I wonder if he's still alive.
Then I hear a snort
and the snoring starts
and I lie back,
my heart beating fast.

I remember

I've started to remember before Mum was ill
we used to go and see the latest films,
we used to eat out
          and go ten-pin bowling.
I remember before Mum was ill
we used to sit together at mealtimes
and Dad would try new recipes on us,
    wonderful smells and tastes:
lamb and cardamom curry, chicken satay.
I remember before Mum was ill
we used to take trips,
         to places we'd never been before.
I remember before Mum was ill
we used to do things together.
We used to talk.
We used to,
I remember.

Morning on repeat Day 41

It's morning on repeat.
Broken plates and burnt toast,
Nana Q being scatty,
rummaging in her bag,
hurrying me along.
She doesn't want me to
be late to school. 'I don't even want to go,'
I say.
'Stop being silly,' she says.
I'm not being silly; I don't
want to go.
I never want to go. I used to.
I just don't want to see anyone,
not now.
Then she hands me a plate
with a slightly squashed
sausage sandwich
and she insists
I eat
all of it
on the way to school.

School day

Today is a school day.
I wake up late
    so I have to run.
I get hot.
    I get sweaty. And I'm coughing.
I can smell my body odour –
it's seeping through my shirt,
    wafting out of my collar.
My face feels red, and I want to turn back.
Everyone has gone in by the time I've crossed the playground.
I see my class through the ground-floor windows.
It feels like they are all staring.
It always feels like everyone is staring.
My eye catches Daisy's
and I wonder if she just feels
sorry for me.

Am I the eggshell?

Am I the eggshell
that no one wants to walk on?
Am I the conversation
that everyone is whispering about?
Am I the subject of their gossip
because I don't want to speak?
Because I just want to hide away
from everyone?

Back to normal

I'm standing by the lockers
when I hear the bell go
and I just want to stay
till everything goes back to normal.
Then I see Daisy and Jade
walking towards me,
and as they get closer
I turn my head
so they won't see me,
and out of the corner of my eye
I notice them turning the other way
and I know they were probably
only trying to help.
Daisy looks back and smiles.
I try smiling back
but it feels pained.

Lunch money

The bell shrills
and it's lunchtime,
but my stomach tightens.
I have no lunch money.
I ask Dan if he'll lend me some…
                    He lends me 30p.
I'm grateful.
30p will do fine.
30p is enough.
I'll pay him back tomorrow.

Invisible

I go and sit by the far side
of the field.
I don't want to be seen,
not today.
Today I want to be invisible
and then maybe for longer –
for a whole day, or a
week...
          a month.
Maybe for ever.

Can anybody help him?

When it's my turn to read
from this term's lit book –
English lit, the only subject
I like –
when it's my turn, Mr Moore
chooses Part Five,
Chapter One.
He chooses me, as I haven't said anything
in a while; I haven't joined in for
a long time.
He chooses me because he knows,
he knows I don't want to be chosen.
Chapter One... Part Five...
The book is *Brighton Rock*
by Graham Greene.
I'm not sure I like it. Another time,
another place, I may like it more,
but not here, not today.
And I have to read it...
out loud, in front of the class.
And it begins
'Everything went well...'
and as I read the words, my throat
dries up, and I feel like I'm
going to retch, and I feel a thin stream,
of vomit form in my mouth.
'Everything went well...'
and I can't continue, so Mr Moore
furthers my embarrassment...

my pain…
my humiliation… my moment in the
dry heat of the sun…

'Everything went well…'
until…
four little words:
'Can anybody help him?'
My failure complete. He moves
to find someone else.
Someone who can do it.

I long for the bell

I long for the bell
to end the day.
Just to hear it ring
brings relief.
They keep saying
it's good for me
to be here
            in this place.
Take my mind off things,
they keep saying.
But they are wrong
and no one listens to me.

After school

Nana Q meets me at the school gate.
She looks worried.
She says she's lost her bag.
Her betting slips,
her football pools,
her lottery tickets,
her loose change,
    her lists...
her endless lists.
I try to calm her
before she starts to cry.

Nana Q's bag

Nana Q looks in the sitting room;
I look in the bedroom.
Nana Q is still crying.
I ask her if she left the house with it.
    Nana Q can't remember.
I ask her when she last saw it.
    Nana Q can't remember.
I hear a tap on the door.
It's Jean.
She has Nana Q's bag.
    Nana Q hugs Jean.
Nana Q is still crying.

Appointment 5 Day 123

We get to the floor with the physio department
just in time to go in.
Freya sits by the bed, her hair now a bright red, like a fire
beginning to roar,
and ushers me over enthusiastically.
'How are you, mate?' she says.
I'm not sure how to answer,
            so I just shrug.
As I lie face down on the bed,
Freya asks me who brought me here.
'My dad,' I say,
'and Nana Q.'
'They visit my mum while we're here.'
Freya goes quiet…
    it's not for long,
but long enough to make it awkward.
Then just as her palm claps against my back,
I hear a faint apology.

Soon on repeat

Soon.
/ suːn /

Adverb.
In a short time,
shortly… presently.
In the future,
before long, in a little while.
In a moment, in a twinkling.
   In a twinkling of an eye…
Before you know it.
Any minute now.
Any day.
By and by.

Going home

I wait by the car.
The wind is blowing hard
and it has started to rain.
I feel like every single part of my body is cold.
What is taking them so long?
My chest feels heavy and sore.
When Nana Q and Dad appear,
they usher me straight into the car.
They don't say anything on the way home
            and I don't ask anything.
It feels better not to.
Nana Q says someone came round
yesterday.
A boy – his name was Dean or Dwayne or something.
'Dan?' I ask
'That's him, nice lad,' she says.
Why did Dan come round?
I'm glad I wasn't there,
I'm not up for seeing anyone,
not right now.

In a second

Whenever we went on long journeys
in the car, we would play a game
where someone would say
a single word and the others
had to think of a song with that
word in the lyrics. Whoever thought
first would have to sing the line.
In the last year or so, I stopped,
I stopped playing.
I stopped wanting to join in.
Mum and Dad would try to
encourage me, but I just tried
to ignore them.
But I know I'd join in now,
today,
this minute.
I'd join in
in a second.

Leftovers

Nana Q scrounges around the kitchen
looking for leftovers.
Some cold chicken,
   baked beans,
    eggs.
There are some potatoes.
They have started sprouting,
the shoots so brittle that they crumble,
spilling dead potato crumbs on the worktop.
Nana Q smiles.
'These will be fine.'

Climb into bed

Right now, I want to climb,
climb into bed, and sleep
and wake up
in another life,
another time,
another me.

Hunting for a lost treasure

Nana Q is on her sofa
where she sleeps,
poring over her
pieces of paper, each one
a fragment of her day, her week,
her month, her year…
her life…
and she's hunting, hunting
for a lost treasure, her privvy.
Her privvy was a special ticket,
a ticket to use on the train,
a privilege ticket, her privvy.
She wanted to find it, not to use it,
but just to know where it is.

The Tube

Nana Q used to work
on the London Underground – the Tube,
that's what she's always called it.
On the Tube she'd be
checking tickets,
talking to people, helping them
find their destination, where to change,
how to change.
She often tells me about a night,
a night when she found a young boy
asleep just by the ticket office
near the Victoria line.
She often tells me that she
woke him up and she made him a cup
of tea… and gave him a biscuit.
He told her he'd run away,
run away from home.
Nana Q phoned the police,
but when they came to get him
he burst into tears.
He wanted to stay with Nana Q
because she'd been so kind.
Nana Q never found out what happened
to the boy. She always wonders
and tells the story all the time.
It always changes a little.
But every time she does,
I see a tear form in her eye.

Dead potatoes and baked beans

Dad has got to go out.
Dead potatoes and baked beans
are not enough to entice Dad to stay.
As he puts his coat on I lie to my dad
that I'm doing a survey for a school project.
It's called
     'How much time does your parent spend with you?'
Dad just looks through me.
He didn't get it
or he didn't hear it.
I want to shout at him.
Scream at him.
Pull at his hair.
  Scratch at his face.
Then I just want to grab him,
wrap my arms and legs around him.
Squeeze out every bit of air between
him and me
and never let go.
I still don't think it would be enough.

Souvenir

Sometimes I *think* it's me.
Sometimes I *know* it's me.
The unwanted souvenir
from a forgettable holiday.
The memento of another time
when things felt comfortable,
                secure,
                        undamaged.
I'm different from
the me before.
Sometimes I *think* it's me.
Sometimes I *know* it's me.
Every day I squeeze my eyes tight,
hoping that when I open them
everything will have changed,
  everything will be all right.

Midnight on repeat

I hear the front door.
It must be midnight —
that's when he comes home.
That's when the pub closes.
Nowhere left to go to hide,
nowhere left to go to drink.
He never drinks at home.
I hear the sound of keys.
It must be midnight.
It must be time for his retreat.
I ignore the clock —
I know what time it is.
It's midnight on repeat and
Dad is downstairs, fumbling around
in the dark, looking a fool,
a clown.
I turn over
and try to sleep.
But I can't; I can hear him
clattering about,
putting the TV on,
turning the volume up
12
14
16
18
20
22.

The volume going up and up in
even numbers. The sound of twenty-four-hour news
blaring out from the box.
Then I hear Nana Q
and I know an argument
is about to start.

A little soggier than the last

It's raining on the way to school
and even before I've reached
the end of the street, my feet
are soaked.
The sole of my shoe is flapping
at the heel.
The cushion punctured, spitting out
the air, letting in the rain.
Again
   and again, and again,
each step a little soggier than the last.
The day feels long
before it's even begun.

Maths

The day begins with maths.
I hate maths –
numbers appear strange.
I try to see what Dan has written,
but he huddles over his work.
A poster to the right
of the board says,
'Three out of two people
have trouble with fractions!'
Mrs Martell catches my eye
    and gestures for me to carry on working.
I feel like I have forgotten how.
I spot Daisy out of the corner
of my eye and she's whispering
something to Jade,
and I wonder if they are talking about me.

Lead her home

Nana Q meets me outside school.
She is upset.
She is shaking.
She is frantic.
She says Dad
has sold the washing machine.
She says he has sold the tumble dryer.
I try to calm her down
and get her to explain again.
She starts to cry
and stumbles on her words.
I take her arm
and lead her home.
I tell her again that Dad isn't working,
that Mum had the job.
She starts to remember
as I lead her home.

Gaps

The kitchen looks strange
with gaps under the worktops.
Nana Q is scrubbing the floor
where the machines used to be.
The warm water in the bowl
beside her has turned a murky grey.
Nana Q is calm now;
she says she'll go to the launderette
first thing in the morning.
She keeps saying it was just the shock,
that's why she was upset.
Just the shock.
'He must have a good reason,' she says.
'It'll all be fine.'
The gaps under the worktop
are shimmering now.
Shimmering ruptures of a wound
that Nana Q is cleaning.

Tired

I'm tired.
Not sleepy tired,
just tired.
Tired of everything.

Playlist

I lie on my bed, listening
to music, a playlist I made myself.
Music to escape,
music to drown out my thoughts,
songs that don't remind me
of things from before.
Songs to distract
and embrace.
Songs that don't matter,
songs to change the way
I feel.
But I find I can't drown out my thoughts
for long.

Dad always liked a drink

Dad always liked a drink.
At home,
in the pub,
at a party.
No one ever really
saw it as anything more
than liking a drink, not
loving a drink, not like now.
Now, when I never get to see him,
now when I need him the most.

The Pause

Not going to school

I leave the house early,
slipping past Nana Q
as she clatters in the kitchen.
I'm not going to school.
I don't feel like it.
I don't suppose anyone will notice.
I head to the park
and find shelter
in the porch of the football club.
It's raining;
light, quiet
sounds patter on the roof
overhead. I count them
and the rhythm takes me away
from my thoughts
and I shut my eyes.
I could stay here for hours.
In this porch of the football club,
in this shelter
where no one can see me,
where no one knows
I exist.
Not going to school
was the best decision
I've made in a long time.

I need to stay well

Sitting here and
my chest feels tight again.
Just sitting here
and my heart starts pounding.
I'm thinking about the symptoms
over and over again in my head.
Tightness, heartbeat, tightness, coughing, tightness,
tightness, tightness, coughing, heartbeat, dizzy, tired,
tightness…
tightness.
I need to stay well.
My legs ache,
so does my head.
I hope this is just a blip,
just an off day.
I need to stay well.
I need to stay well to see Mum.
I think about Freya.
I think about her smile
and the way she speaks to me
and my heart seems to calm and
my chest seems to ease.
I need to stay well for Mum,
for Freya.

Bad   Day 130

There are days when
I think I should wonder about Mum,
but all I can think of is Freya, when
I should be thinking about Mum,
and I feel bad.

We arrive early,
just Nana Q and me.
We didn't hear from Dad.
I think about running,
running to Mum's room.
No one to stop me.
No one to tell me what to do.
But I know I can't,
I know that I could make it worse.
I see Freya.
She comes out to call me in.
'Hey, mate? How's it going?'
she says, her hair up in a bun
on the top of her head, her darker roots showing through, with
    the tips a vibrant purple.
Her tunic splattered with blue and green paint.
'I did a bit of painting at the weekend,
got a bit carried away!' she says.
She's always so happy,
so full of life,
like no one I know.
Today it's
thoracic expansion exercises.
I lie on my side.
'Let's clear that inferior segment!'
she says, like a football coach
preparing a team.

I raise my foot
and repeat… and repeat
and I cough
and wheeze and cough again.
She lies me back,
a pillow under my back for
postural drainage,
my favourite.
And I can feel it coming out,
my little green joy.
And the routine comes to an end.
I feel so much better
but I still have to keep
coming back – it's not all gone,
not yet.

Canberra

Freya tells me she's from Canberra
in the district of Woden Valley.
She's lived there all her life
till now.
I've lived here all my life,
I say.
I was born in this hospital,
my second home.
Born here,
grew up here,
probably die here
in this place,
in this hospital.
Woden Valley, she tells me,
is named after the god
of wisdom, an old English god.
Freya tells me there are a lot
of bush fires near where she lived.
I could listen to her for hours.
Everything sounds like a story,
a novel,
a poem.
I want to know it all.
She tells me how in her street
if anyone is alone for the night
the other residents leave their lights on
like a beacon,

so they feel safe.
So they don't feel alone, but...
soon our time is up and I just want to hear more.

I wish

I wish I could stay here
right now
in this moment
with Freya,
where I don't feel
like a stranger
even though I'm with Freya.
I wish I could stay
with her.

Ritual

Nana Q has a ritual
on a Saturday morning.
She heads into town
pulling her bogie behind her.
She first goes to the newsagent's
where she buys five different newspapers.
The *Sun*.
The *Mail*.
The Times.
The *Guardian*.
And *Sporting Life* to check
the horse-racing forms.
She then buys two lottery tickets
and a football pools coupon.
'You can help me with that,'
she says enthusiastically.
I tell her I can't wait,
as she shoves a pencil
in my hand
then places the pools coupon
on the table in front of me.
'Score draws, pet,
tick the ones you think will
be score draws,' she says.
I look at the coupon
and just tick the numbers
I like.

Ritual 2

When Nana Q has finished
at the newsagent's, she requires rest,
a cup of tea and time
to fill out her betting slips
before the eleven o'clock at Epsom.
We go to a coffee shop
next door to the newsagent's.
Nana Q orders two teas.
I hate tea.
And two slices of Battenberg cake.
I hate Battenberg cake.
'Eat up,' Nana Q says
as she fumbles in her bag
for a pen.
Just then, out of the corner of my eye,
I see a familiar face.
I see a familiar smile.

Unexpected guest

Freya picks up her cup
and wanders over to our table.
'Can I join you?' she asks.
I timidly nod.
'Is this your gran?'
Freya asks, pointing at Nana Q.
I nod again.
'I'm his nana,' Nana Q corrects her.
'Now hold these, please.'
Nana Q hands Freya a pile
of betting slips
    then proceeds to open up
her copy of *Sporting Life* fully
across the table.
I place a piece of Battenberg
in my mouth,
        and pretend I can't taste the marzipan.
Freya whispers in my ear,
'What is she doing?'
Nana Q sniffs and pops her head
from behind the paper: 'I'm checking the form, dear.'

Checking the form

Nana Q says the art of checking the form
for horse racing is based
on a number of factors.
The Going.
This is the condition of the surface
that the horses run on.
Hard, Firm, Good to Firm,
Good, Soft, Good to Soft.
The Going is accessed by moisture,
    moisture in the ground.
And dirt
and turf
and density
and porosity
and compaction.
Nana Q checks them all.
The Track.
Is it tight?
Is it wide?
Weights.
If the horse is a good horse,
it has to carry more weight, to make it fair.
More weight, so the bad horses can catch up.
Nana Q checks this.
Nana Q checks it all.

Be good

Freya smiles,
and I can't think of anything to say.
'You not hungry?' she says,
lifting up my plate with
the half-eaten Battenberg.
'Not really,' I say.
Freya picks up the cake
and shoves it into her mouth,
then continues to talk.
'The cakes are great in this place –
have you tried the lemon drizzle?'
I shake my head.
'Maybe next time, eh?'
Freya gets up to leave.
'I'll see you again soon, mate.'
By the door she shouts,
'Be good!' just like Nana Q sometimes does.
I wonder what she means,
be good?

Ritual 3

Nana Q charges, slips in hand,
straight to the betting shop.
I can't go in.
I wait in the doorway, clinging
to Nana Q's trolley.
There is a multicoloured
door curtain that blows back
and forth, each time
revealing the contents inside.
Nana Q is scribbling furiously, her slips
getting jumbled by the flurry of people
brushing back and forth.
I turn back to look at the street.
We'll be going home soon.
This is what I tell myself.

Appointment 7 Day 137

She greets me with
a smile, as she does each time.
I feel warm, I feel better.
But I don't want this to end.
But it will.
It has to... doesn't it?
We talk about the weather, TV programmes
and school. Freya calls it
'shooting the shit!' when you talk
about surface stuff, common ground,
passing the time.
She says sometimes it's easier,
not to dig deeper –
clap... as her hand meets my back –
to find out too much.
Clap...
She says sometimes when you do
Clap...
get to know someone, you find out
Clap...
how you don't know each other
at all.
Clap...
At all.

Leviathan

As soon as one appointment finishes
I start to think to the next.
I start to think about seeing her
again,
seeing her smile
again.
It builds in my mind
and takes me away,
away from everything else.
Away from my thoughts, my
rotten, putrid, anxious thoughts.
They coil and twist like a leviathan,
a monster, a beast, a creature from
the deep. But with her
I hear songs, I hear laughter,
I hear things I haven't heard
for so many hours...
days...
weeks...
months...
till Freya.

Sharing our secrets

I keep thinking about Freya,
how I should have talked to her,
told her what was going on.
I just felt like I could.
I felt like I wanted to.
It just seemed right somehow.
Maybe she would have something
to tell me,
   some secret she hasn't told anyone.
Sharing our stories,
    sharing our secrets.
I keep thinking Freya
would understand, she would care.
If I told her it all,
every... single... bit,
she'd know what to say.
She'd know what to say
to make me feel better.
I keep thinking Freya
might have heard this
kind of stuff before, that
she could give me some
advice, help me know
how to feel, how to be.
    Sharing our stories,
sharing our secrets.

Something

I wonder if we all
carry something sad inside us
that no one else can see.
Something we do not mention,
something we hope will leave
and never come back.

I hope she hears me

There are times
when people talk to me
and I don't hear them.
I don't, even though they are there.
But not with Freya.
I always hear her.
I always see her.
I hope she hears me.

Washing machine

We pass by the Old Phoenix shop.
It sells all sorts of junk, odds and ends,
electrical equipment.
In the window I see a washing machine.
Our washing machine.
Nana Q tugs on my coat.
'Let's get home,' she says.
'Let's get home.'

Hard to sleep

I look over at the clock: it says
4.15 a.m.
My chest feels tight, each breath
is painful. It feels like it did before,
when the infection first started.
I cough and it's dry and unproductive.
Every dry cough feels like a failure.
I turn from one side
   to the other, then back again.
I look over at the clock: it says
4.54 a.m.
I'm feeling every minute tonight,
every second.
4.55, 4.56, 4.57.
Turn from one side to the other,
then back again.
Every minute, every second.
4.58, 4.59, 5.00.
Chest sore – check.
Coughing – check.
Feeling exhausted – check.
Ready to give up – check.
One side to the other,
then back again.
5.01, 5.02, 5.03.
Every minute.
Every second.

Sometimes I wish

Sometimes I wish it was Dad
    in the hospital.
Sometimes I wish it was Dad being
described in overheard conversations.
I wish it was Dad that
was
    dying.
It would be easier that way.
Sometimes I wish it was Dad
connected to tubes and wires.
I wish it was Dad that
couldn't sit up,
  couldn't wipe his own mouth.
It would be better that way.
Sometimes I wish it was Dad
just lying there, with his skin looking like
it's being pierced by his bones.
I wish it was Dad yelling out to the nurse
to stop the pain,
    to take it away.
It would be simpler that way.
Sometimes I wish it was Dad
with thin and fragile hair
and nosebleeds that last for hours.
I wish it was Dad trying to smile with cracked lips.
Sometimes I wish it was Dad.
It would be manageable that way.

Forget about getting up

I hear the streets below
as I lie in my bed.
I feel like I'm floating under
the loose covers.
I make a tent, with my legs
propping up the duvet.
I wonder how long it would take to die
if I held my breath.
I can see the sun peering through the gaps
in the curtain; I feel the warmth
on my face.
I decide to turn over.
I decide I want to sleep again
and forget about getting up.

Rituals on repeat

We're on repeat.
Nana Q has to go to town
to the betting shop.
We're on repeat.
Then the newsagent's.
We're on repeat.
I hope we go to the coffee shop.
I really hope we see Freya.
I want to talk to her again.
I want to be on repeat,
spending time with her.
Today repeat is OK.
When we get to the coffee shop
we're the only ones there.
Nana Q has tea.
I have tea.
Nana Q has a blueberry muffin.
I have a coffee and walnut slice.
The door of the shop opens,
the door of the shop shuts.
People come in,
people go out.
But no Freya.
Nana Q flaps around
her slips,
her tickets,
her bag,
and the door opens

and Freya comes in
and I can feel my cheeks
grow warm… blood red.
'Hey you!' she says.
'I wondered if I'd see you today.'
I smile.
She smiles.
Freya joins us and tells me about
her home… the suburbs.
Every year they have a public holiday,
she says,
called Canberra Day, to celebrate
the founding of Canberra.
She tells me about her street
and how the residents come together.
Eat together,
celebrate together.
I say we never have things like that,
only once, when the Queen
had an anniversary for something.
She laughs. 'You guys and your Queen,'
she says, 'always celebrating her for something.'
I tell her about my home,
how I like it,
how I like living near the sea,
and we agree, it's a nice place
to live.

'Or die,'
I say.
She makes a half smile,
            an uncomfortable smile,
and then says she has to go,
and she's gone before
I can say,
'I didn't mean to say that.'

It started with a fever

It started with a fever,
then night sweats.
One day she was fine, and then she wasn't.
High levels of white blood cells.
Sickness, tiredness, pain.
Low levels of red blood cells.
Bruises, stomachaches, nosebleeds.
That's how it started.
One day she was fine, and then she wasn't.
Her body started fighting itself.
Mouth sores, blood counts, chemo.
Pain, burning like a fire inside.
One day she was fine, and then she wasn't.

Relief   Day 145

It's 5.16 a.m.
My bladder starts to pinch. I want
to sleep, I need to sleep.
I want to put off going to the toilet, but
I keep thinking about it and
the feeling won't go away.
I go to move the duvet
to get up,
to move.
And I can't hold it any more,
and it's such a relief.
I can't stop and
I don't want it to stop, and when it does,
I just turn over.

Running late

I leave the house.
It's cold
… I'm late.
I see the train pulling into the station.
I think about running.
But I don't.
As I cross the green
the football club is on my left.
No one is around, so I sit on the porch again.
The wind whistles around me, but I feel protected
in that doorway, with no one around.
I'll say I missed the train.
I'll say I had an appointment.
This is the plan I make
in my head.

Blackbird

I like the peace of this place.
I can't hear anything.
It's still.
It's calm.
A blackbird trots along the floor
right in front of me.
It doesn't notice me
sitting here, staring.
It doesn't care; it's looking
for something to eat, listening
for worms under the ground,
waiting for them to make
… a move.
It peers intensely at the grass.
I wonder, has it heard something
moving,
wriggling?
It reminds me of
listening out for Dad,
peering at the clock,
waiting to hear some movement.
Suddenly the blackbird swivels
and stares right up at me
sitting here,
where he's hunting.
An intruder.
We look each other in the eye.

Its yellow eye ring
looks stark and cold, like glass,
and as I start to look away
it moves to keep my gaze,
as if it recognises me.
I gently move my hand forward
towards it, but as I do,
it turns and flies away.
I soon lose sight of it and return my gaze
to the porch in front of me.
And I feel alone again
and I feel haunted.

Double English

By the time I get in
my class has double English.
Everyone is reading a book.
The Diary of a Young Girl
by Anne Frank.
In the introduction Anne expresses
her want,
       … her need
for a true friend.
A friend she can confide in,
a friend she can share all her
innermost thoughts with.
There is no one here
I can do that with,
who I want to talk to.
Just her,
just Freya.

Washing them in the sink

As I come through the door,
I hear Nana Q in the bathroom.
As I walk in, I see she's washing my sheets.
She's washing my pyjamas.
She's washing them in the sink.
With hand soap…
with warm water, warm soapy water.
She's happy.
Fulfilling her duties.
A grandmother…
A mother…
I feel a little warm inside.
A feeling of ease,
relief, clean clothes and sheets
are all I want right now.

Nana G

I used to have another nana.
Nana G died when I was five.
I don't remember Nana G,
but Nana Q says I'm like her.
Nana G and Nana Q were very different.
I hope I'm a bit like them both.

Terminal

They told me while we ate dinner.
We were in a restaurant,
one of those gourmet burger places
where they stack the burgers high
and poke a stick through them
so they don't topple over.
Like it was a treat,
a treat for me
before I gain the knowledge
of Mum's condition.
And when they said it –
the word
… terminal –
I felt like that burger,
the word like a stick piercing
into me
… terminal.
Two years, four years, could be six years,
maybe more, depending on treatments,
but… terminal.

I'm thinking about Freya,
when I see her from across the street.
She looks at me then waves.
Her just knowing me, recognising me
feels like a victory.
She wanders over to me, and I don't
look away once, watching each step she takes.
Each one feels like a breath I'm taking: in… step,
out… step,

      … in… step,

out…
step.
And then she arrives in front of me, and
I can't think of anything to say.
'Hey, how are you doing?' she says.
'OK – you?' I reply, trying to act
nonchalant, but not like a dick.
Not like someone who thinks too much
of themselves. But I think she knows that.
She says she's heading to the local
museum; she wants to find out more
about the town.
'Do you want to come?' she asks,
and I'm screaming inside, I'm
bursting.
'Yes, please, if you don't mind,'
I say.
I say, hoping she doesn't, hoping it's

not just because she feels sorry for me.
But because she really wants me to
come too. And as we walk together
I feel my heart beat in time with every
single one of her steps.

At the museum

The museum is near the beach.
It's based inside an old tower –
a Martello tower. The Martello tower.
A fort, a defensive fort, from
the nineteenth century.
The lady at the counter is old and
frail; I wonder if she is from
the nineteenth century.
Freya pays for us and we
walk down the spiral stairs.

Hair and shoes

I study Freya's hair as we descend
the stairs,
further and further down. Curving round
and I'm trying not to get dizzy, looking
at her hair...
... now bleach blonde,
bleach blonde, with hints of honey
dripping over sand.
A desert.
And her shoes, they are orange,
bright orange, with pink laces,
the sort of shoes that would look silly
on anyone else, but she can pull them off.
But she can, she makes them look cool.
She's cool. I think I might be dreaming.

Local world

I remember coming here
when I was young,
just with Dad.
Just the two of us, finding
out about the local world.
About where we are from
about where we were then.

Olivetti Lettera 32

Freya beckons me over; she
has seen a room full of old machines and
gadgets.
We look at old wind-up phones; they look
so strange, unusable,
unfamiliar. We look at an old typewriter.
It's blue… an Olivetti,
Olivetti Lettera 32. It looks
like it's from another time, another
world. I laugh and show Freya.
'Look at this old thing!'
She looks at it but doesn't speak.
She doesn't laugh.
She stands looking at it.
'My dad had one of these,' she says.
'He was a writer,
a journo, for the local newspaper.
He bloody loved that typewriter.'
I feel like I've said the wrong thing.
I feel my face flush and I look at my shoes, and I feel my legs
twitching
nervously.

Looking back

Freya sees an old cine projector.
The sign says it's from 'The Ritz',
a cinema that used to be where the
local supermarket now stands.
So many changes in one small place,
so many faces,
so many people and times and things, just
in this one place.
I look at Freya
and she's looking back at the typewriter.

Private island

Freya tells me about
a film she watched the night before,
where the main character
described wanting to look for
a private island,
a place to run away to.
Freya tells me about how she
had lost her
dad two years ago
    … in a car accident.
She said everything reminded her
of him, everything had a memory,
everything felt painful.
So she packed up her things
and flew to England.
She was looking for a private island.
Somewhere no one knew her.
Where she wouldn't see things…
things that would remind her of him.
A private island where pain
and loss can't find you,
where you can hide in the landscapes,
in the buildings, the trees,
the beaches,
the sights…
the sounds.
But you can't outrun grief; it
always catches up with you

in the end.
Sometimes you just have to embrace it,
hold it tight,
then wring its neck.

The lights

I remember before we moved,
before Mum was ill,
every Saturday morning
we would go to the cinema.
We'd share a bucket of popcorn,
which we would finish
before the film started.
When the lights went down,
I would look over at my parents.
Mum would be leaning her head
on Dad's shoulder,
and they would be holding hands.
Everything felt right.
Everything felt comfortable.
I remember stepping out
of the cinema after the film
and thinking the world looked so different,
everything looked so vivid,
everything looked so alive.
It was the morning after one such trip
that Mum woke up feeling dizzy
and nothing would be the same again.
Freya puts her hand
on my hand
and squeezes
a little bit. Just enough
to bring me back

from this memory,
just enough
to make me smile.

I head into the physio room

I head into the physio room.
I feel a little giddy.
I want to see her again,
to talk again, like we did
before.
But something is different.
I head into the physio room
and it's not the same.
I head into the physio room
and a man is sitting by the desk.
I head into the physio room
and…
Freya isn't there…
Replaying it all,
I replay Freya and I
sitting in the coffee shop,
replaying what I said,
                what I did,
replaying it all.
Had grief caught her up?
Had it found her
and started to bare its teeth?
I feel like asking
where she is
but I feel nervous
all of a sudden
and I wish I could just
turn and leave.

The grey wig

I remember when Mum
went to buy a wig;
her hair was dropping out.
She chose a grey one.
She didn't have grey hair –
it was dark
like a night sky.
But she wanted grey,
like she wanted to look older,
frailer, different
or disguised.
Like she wanted to be someone else,
look like someone else,
be someone else. I hated that wig,
that storm-cloud-grey wig
that made my mum
look like someone else.
Not my mum
any more.

Throw up

I feel like throwing up
so much more than usual.
I never want to throw up
when Freya is here.

Forcing

Clapping under my arms,
my back,
    my chest.
It feels rougher than usual.
A masculine touch
forcing out that little green spit,
not easing it out
    ... like Freya does.
And when it plops into the cup
it doesn't feel so triumphant.
I feel cheated.

Cheat

V. cheat·ed, cheat·ing, cheats,
deprive of something expected,
deprive,
trick… swindle,
an act of cheating.
I feel angry.
I feel afraid.
I hope I haven't lost her.

Confetti

Back in the waiting room
Nana Q is sorting and shuffling
through her slips and papers.
All strewn across
the waiting-room table,
like pieces of confetti lying
at the feet of a happy couple
on their wedding day.
I know she sees my eyes.
My watery eyes.
She gathers up her papers
and without saying anything
we leave.

The only one I want to see

I think about Freya.
I think about how she made me feel.
I think about whether I'll see her again.
I think about the things I want to tell her,
all about everything.
I want to tell her
all about everything.
She's the only one I want to see,
the only one I want to speak to.
I sit in my room
leaving lights on
like a beacon.

I keep telling myself Day 149

Nana Q takes me to the café.
Nana Q thinks we might see Freya again.
I hope Nana Q is right.
I keep telling myself.

Nana Q takes me to the café.
Nana Q thinks Freya will be there.
I hope Nana Q is right.

Nana Q takes me to the café.
Nana Q thinks we will see Freya again.

Nana Q takes me to the café.
Nana Q thinks she'll be there next time.

The kitchen is hot

The kitchen is hot.
The water is boiling over
and bubbling up out of the top
of the saucepan.
Nana Q and Dad are in the other room.
Dad is shouting at Nana Q.
Nana Q is crying.
I turn the hob down and the
fire alarm starts to ring out.
I waft a tea towel around
to disperse the steam, and I hear
the front door slam.

Betting-slip confetti

Nana Q sits on the floor
in the hallway
surrounded by bits of paper
like confetti
made of torn-up
betting slips and
lottery tickets.
I go to help, but
Nana Q doesn't look at me
as she pushes me away.
It takes her two hours to
finally let me help,
to help her gather her
betting-slip confetti.

Clinging

The front door reopens
and the clock says 1 a.m.
I'm still awake.
Dad stumbles up the stairs.
I come out of my room to see him
clinging to the banister.
Clinging to a bottle
before pausing and swigging,
trying to drink away
how he feels.
He looks up at me
then glances to the wall.
A picture.
In a frame.
A picture in a frame
of my mum.
A younger mum
        … a forgotten mum.
His fingertips caress the glass,
trying to touch the face behind.
And then he slips.
And the picture drops.
It all happens so fast.
Smashed,
smashed and cracked
and splinters of glass
        … on the stair.

He screams
and he yells at me
and he blames me.
I think he wants for me
what I want for him.
To be the one that's ill.
I turn and run back
                ... back to my room.
That's when I decide to leave.

Time changes everything

Time changes everything.
When I was younger,
my dad and I
pretended to be wrestlers,
like the American wrestlers
we used to watch on TV.
We'd set out the living room
to look like the ring, and
my dad would pick me up,
spin me round his head,
then throw me on the sofa. When
I tried to stand up, he'd throw me
back down. I laughed harder than
I ever have before or since.
Before or since.
Time changes everything.

Leaving Day 150

I leave the house.
It's 5 a.m. I have a bag.
I have water, crisps,
a jumper.
No one hears me leave.
Outside the sun shines.
The day begins.
The day begins for me.

Moving

I see people moving
but they aren't looking.
I walk against the traffic,
against the grain of the
busy commute.
My nose starts to tickle, to itch.
I try to hold off a sneeze,
but it explodes, all over
the passing traffic of people.
But they don't flinch,
they don't stop or ignore
where they are going.
Swarms of people, all heading
in the opposite direction.
The opposite direction...

                    to me.

The beach

I sit on the beach
watching the tide
coming in…
        going out.
I see a swimmer in the sea,
and I imagine myself swimming too.
The ice-cold ocean grazing my face,
my arms,
  my legs.
I shiver…
        I cough.
From the beach
I see the ocean in all its magnificence.
Waves curling and hitting the shore.
I imagine walking out
… into the sea
before stepping inside the horizon.
Leaving it all behind.

As my friend

I think about Freya
and how I miss her.
Or at least the idea of her
as my friend…

And it aches.

Another life

I think about if I was bad
in another life.
If in another life
I was cruel... I was unfair,
unjust... uncaring.
I think about if in another life
I hurt someone,
and if I did, that I'm
paying for it now.
That I was so horrible
that life is paying me back.
That is why, that is why
these things are happening
to me...
to us.

Closer to the water

I wander out across
the shingled beach.
It's difficult to navigate
and I walk like a drunk.
In the darkness
the half-moon guides me
closer to the water
and I hear the waves gently
brushing the shore.
It feels like it's beckoning me
and I respond by tentatively
moving closer,
then closer…
        until I feel the water lap over my feet.
I pause
and wonder if I should stay here,
let the waves take me,
swallow me up.
What would people say?
Would I be missed?
I know it would remove
the pain I feel right now.
But as I am thinking about these
things, I find that the tide
has retreated
and my feet feel the stones
beneath me again…

I wander back up the beach
believing that the sea has
helped to make my decision
to stay, just as
the coldness of the moment
kicks in.

Memorial benches

I notice as I walk
how many memories
there are on benches
        ... how much loss.
In loving memory of...
                Our every prayer
to Alice Arnold 1915–1982,
    to Jack Butters 1907–2001,
to Elizabeth Penny 1935–2014,
    to Henry Mandrake 1954–2009.
I wonder who they are,
these lost lives with their scorecards.
And for a moment I feel griefless.
And I start to feel guilty.
In loving memory of...
                Our every prayer
to Sidney Chalmers 1927–1992,
    to Susan Bowles 1965–1995,
to Roy Sullivan 1955–2003,
    to Diane Simpson 1947–2011.
So many lives,
so much loss.

Beach hut

The wind is cold,
so I find a spot by an old
beach hut. To hide,
to rest, to sleep.
My chest feels tight.
And for the first time today
I think about Mum.

Good things and rubber rings

We used to walk along this beach
when I was little. We'd play
at throwing big stones in the sea
to see who could make
the loudest plop.
We'd turn up our trousers
and paddle in the sea.
It was always cold. Dad
used to say at the end of the summer
the water would warm up.
It never did.
We'd pack a picnic of sandwiches,
cream cheese and pickle, tomatoes
and lettuce.
Good things and rubber rings was
the thing we used to say.
We used to say.
But not for a long time; the words
now feel like a foreign language.
I remember them, but
I don't recognise them.
We used to walk along this beach
at weekends, after Saturday shopping,
after Sunday lunches.
Whenever we could.
It seems like someone else's life,
not mine, I don't recognise it,
not any more.

We used to walk along this beach,
Mum, Dad and me,
even Nana Q sometimes.
Nana Q would wander slowly behind
chatting to everyone she met. Mum
and Dad would just whisper in
each other's ears, giggling as
they walked along. I would walk in front
kicking stones as if they were footballs,
scoring goals with each and every kick.
We used to walk along this beach
in another time,
when I was little.

Storm

I feel a storm, it's coming.
A natural disturbance, a force.
Wind,
rain,
thunder, lightning, the atmosphere
raging. I feel it,
I feel its anger; I know
that anger.
And it will attack, just like
thoughts attack a mind.
My mind, like a storm, raging
and angry.

Wooden bed with wooden pillows

Wooden bed with wooden pillows,
this is where I am at.
This is my comfort for
the night.
Thoughts start to queue up
in my mind, one
behind another,
but they're not waiting patiently, each trying to bustle past
the other,
each trying to have the first word.
It's relentless,
it's tiring,
but they won't let me sleep
here on this
wooden bed with
wooden pillows.

Come round

As I start to come round
I see a woman
leaning over me.
She asks if I can hear her.
I nod, then she places
an oxygen mask over my face.
To my left a small crowd
gathers to see what's going on.
My chest feels heavy, like
someone is sitting on it.
The woman puts a blanket
over my shoulder and guides
me over to a waiting ambulance.
I ask for my bag.
I want my bag.

Dazed

Dad stands at the end of the bed.
Head bowed, his body still.
Nana Q is sitting in the corner
of the room,
rustling in her bag.
  Rustling in her bag and
mumbling to herself.
I feel tired,
I feel dazed.
Dad moves round to the side
and drags a chair up to the bed.
The sound of it scraping makes
me cringe.
Dad sits, takes my hand and
says he thought he'd lost me too.

One hundred and fifty-two days ago

The day Mum went into
hospital, I thought it wouldn't
be for long.
I didn't think it would be
for ever.
It seemed like any other day.
I got ready for school; Nana Q
was taking me.
I said goodbye
one hundred and fifty-two days ago.
She whispered something to me,
something I still can't figure out.
One hundred and fifty-two days ago.
Dad came to the door. He said,
'It's time.' Mum smiled, we all smiled.
One hundred and fifty-two days ago.
I think it will for ever feel like yesterday.
It might keep her closer to me.

Letting go

The door opened and the room
sucked me in.
Dad said it's OK.
It's OK for me to go in now,
I won't cause any damage now.
Machines bleeped and whirred.
A large fan beat its wings in the corner
and a nurse excused herself from the room.
Dad gripped my hand tightly;
I could see the white of his knuckles.
I could see his irises looking drained
of colour,
       of life.
Mum lay on the bed,
still, eyes closed, mouth slightly open,
breathing, but not alive.
Tubes and wires came from
many directions, and we moved
carefully to our positions:
me one side, my dad the other.
I wanted to touch her,
I wanted to hold her,
I wanted to breathe life into her.
Dad leaned in, kissed her cheek
and whispered something
into her ear before withdrawing.
Right now, I'd be anywhere else but here.
Right now, I'd do anything else but this.

Letting go,
     seeing her let go.
I think of Freya
and Nana Q.
I think of Dad, and I realise
his pain, I understand.
For the first time I understand.
I grab Mum's hand and I squeeze it.
I want to revive her, bring her back,
and I call to her, and I start to scream
and it hurts so much.
My dad comes over. He holds me
and he keeps saying he's sorry.
Over and over again.

The moment

The moment Mum died
the nurse was in the room,
and she listened to Mum's
heart, then checked her eyes
with a small torch.
As she stood back she
nodded to my dad, and
we both knew she'd gone.
We both knew it wasn't Mum
lying there any more.
Her skin seemed to tighten
and pale before us.
It felt like we'd all been
holding our breath for one hundred
and fifty-two days and now
we had all breathed out
at the same time.
And we all felt the relief.

The Warmth

The first thing I see

Nana Q sits in the waiting room.
I'm staring at her as she writes
on a piece of paper, when
I feel a tap on my shoulder.
I turn around and the first thing I see
is her smile.
            It's Freya.
As we sit in the waiting room,
Freya puts her hand
on my hand
and squeezes it a little.
            Just enough
to make me smile.

Her hand is like a portal

Her hand is like a portal
pulling me in...
pulling me free
of the place I was in.
The place where I couldn't breathe.
The place where I was suffocating.
Her hand
holding mine,
comforting and warm.
Neither of us says anything.
We don't need to.
Perhaps we've never needed to.
Her hand,
my hand,
and release.

A memory to visit

Now I have a memory
to visit, a memory to
go to
in the night
when I'm awake.
I can visit this moment.
Nothing can take it away. Seeing Mum
and saying goodbye.

Moments

Mo·ment:
a brief, indefinite interval of time.
Life is just a bunch
of moments, thoughts, sights
and sounds.
And if there is something
I now know that
I didn't know before, it's that
every single one
is precious. Every single one
is real…
                    is mine.
Moments, a point in time
that is mine, to remember
for good,
for bad,
but mine.

Going home 2

Dad sits next to me in the back
of the taxi; Nana Q is in the front
talking at the driver and fiddling with her purse.
We're going home.
We're going to start over.
Nana Q starts hollering at the driver
to pull over,
      to stop.
We're outside the Old Phoenix shop.
Nana Q scrambles out of the taxi
and heads inside.
Two minutes later she's back
inside the car, asking the driver
if there is room for a washing machine.
Nana Q never wins.
But Nana Q has won.

We walk united

The church is full.
People to the left,
people to the right.
The stained-glass windows
reflecting the light, and it changes and moves
and dances as we take each step.
The saints on either side of us,
watching us, judging us.
And
I'm carrying a single rose,
a red rose.
I can smell its strong perfume
and I can feel one of its
sharp thorns.
I'm supposed to
place the rose,
this single red rose,
on the casket,
but I'm not sure, I'm not sure
I can do it.
The people to the left
and the people to the right
are watching on.

After the funeral

I sit in the living room
with a plate of food:
sausage rolls, vol-au-vents, crisps,
pineapple and cheese on sticks,
like a party, with everyone in black,
everyone pretending to be having
a time – not a nice time, just a time.
I see Nana Q rustling in her bag,
her betting slips falling through
the cracks in her fingers, onto
the floor.
All around me I hear quiet chat,
pleasantries, niceties, whatever you
want to call them.
I hear them saying,
'At least she's no longer in pain,'
and,
'She battled till the end,'
and,
'It was a beautiful service.'
And I don't remember any of these
people being around.
I don't remember any of these people
coming to see us.
I hear some of these people
talk about how they knew her,
how they knew her personally,
or how they thought they knew her.

But I don't recognise the person
they describe, and I hear some
people whisper.
They whisper about my dad,
about how he hasn't coped,
about how we needed help,
but I don't remember any of these people,
I don't remember any of them
coming to see us.
I look at my plate of food
and I look at the people
around the room, and the two
begin to blur, both so
insignificant in this moment.
Nana Q is still gathering her things,
and not one single person
tries to help. Right now
I wish Freya was here, just to have
a comrade, someone
who might understand.
But she's not, and I walk over
to help Nana Q.

Another day

I head upstairs
and lie down on my bed. It's been
a long day and my chest feels sore.
The window next to me still has
a border of condensation
round it, and I shut my heavy eyes,
and when I open them again
it's another day.

Looking for a private island

When I see Freya again,
it's at the café. Nana Q had arranged it.
She was going home,
leaving, but she wanted
to say goodbye.
I needed to say goodbye.
The days at the hospital seem
like a blur, and we don't
reminisce, but one day we'll write it down
and send each other letters.
One day
soon.

Our own

We all have our own
private islands.
Places we wish we could escape to,
places we go to in our heads
                     ... in our imaginations.
And for a while
          mine was Freya.
She was mine.
And even though it wasn't real,
she was it...
         my private island.

Finding friends

It was as we left the café,
after I'd said goodbye to Freya,
after she'd hugged me,
                    that I saw them:
    Dan, Luka and Nazim.
They asked who she was,
how we'd met,
was she my girlfriend,
and then
how I'd been
and that they knew
what had happened.
And as they looked at me,
I felt myself grow.
I felt taller.
I felt strong.

Every time

Every time Dad goes out
I worry…
Every time he doesn't come back
when he says he will, I worry…
Will he ever change?
Will I ever trust him, will
he let me trust him?
I wonder if he hides, hides
bottles, a stash of booze.
I try to smell his breath, I try
to check his wallet, I think about
confiscating his money, his cards…
I'm the grown-up, I'm the carer.
But how long can this go on?

Orange-breath rebellion Day 189

He keeps eating oranges
as soon as he gets in.
I think he's trying to cover
his breath.
It's his orange-breath rebellion.

Before Day 1   Day 191

Sometimes he just sits on the sofa,
sometimes he just stays in bed,
sometimes I wonder if he'll
ever come back again,
back to where he was before.
Before Day 1.

Awakenings Day 206

Today there was an awakening,
a stirring from upstairs, movement.
Little steps and the door opens
and closes before I can reach it.
And straight away I think the worst
of him.
I think that's it, he's going to get wet again,
get wet with booze and roll in at midnight.
Midnight on repeat again, again
and again.
Another cycle...
And I wonder if he will ever stop.

Leaflets

Dad walks into
the living room. He has leaflets,
lots of leaflets that the doctor gave him.
Leaflets about help, leaflets of all
shapes and sizes, colours…
so many colours, a rainbow of leaflets
fanned out in front of my eyes, like
he's a magician asking me to pick a card.
I shrug, and he shrugs too.
And he sits and shows me them
one by one.
There is no big fanfare,
no big admission.
He just says,
'I need to change…
I will change.'
Then he takes my hand
and squeezes it.

A start Day 218

Nana Q and I wait in the corridor
just outside the room.
I can see inside
there are eight people
sitting,
sitting and waiting.
Dad is sitting near the back,
like the new kid in school,
knees twitching, eyes darting
around the room.
There's a man in front.
He kind of looks the same,
like you wouldn't know,
like they didn't have a problem
like they weren't addicts.
When the meeting starts
it seems strange;
it's not like in films
when someone stands up
and says they have a problem.
They listen and sometimes
they speak. But Dad,
Dad just listens and listens
and listens
and listens
and watches
and then he spies me
through the glass in the door

and he tries a smile
and I'm sure he has tears
welling in his eyes.
And I know he's made
a start.

Come back

Will I never leave again?
And will I ever trust again?
I'm working on these things,
just like Dad is working
on his things.
We all have things,
these ghosts
that follow us around,
haunting our emotions, our
thoughts,
our choices. Everyone wants to be happy,
have nice things, and friends,
a perfect family, a perfect life.
But we never stop to consider
that these things often
come from pain, from
suffering,
from darkness.
We never stop to consider
the struggles we suffer and
the person we are afterwards.
We never stop to think
how we are defined by
moments of agony
and how we are changed
for ever.
Sometimes you have to go
so far away

to come back again.
I'm not sure where I am,
not right now, but I know
when I do, it might be that
I've started to heal.

Not a choice

On the wall there is a poster:
'Addiction is not a choice!'
I think about how it's easy
for some people to judge others,
to think their struggles are a
choice, that someone would actually
choose to be that way.

Every bugger else

On the way home, I ask
Nana Q if she's OK.
'Oh yes,' she replies.
'It's every bugger else you have
to worry about.'
I laugh, but I know she's
being serious.

The invasion of Sicily

Nana Q tells me at the next meeting
about
her husband,
my grandfather.
She tells me about how
he died in the invasion of Sicily
in World War II.
She tells me about
the last time
she saw him,
standing by their fireplace.
She tells me about
Operation Husky, how the plan
was to land on the
southeastern coast
of the island.
And the last time she saw him
he was standing by their fireplace
and he sang to her; he sang,
and she sang.
She tells me about
how the assaults on the island
would be supported by the navy,
with them landing around midnight
on the tenth day of the month.
And he sang to her, a song.
Nana Q starts to sing.
Nana Q tells me about

the strong wind, a wind
that reached 45 mph, a wind
that blew the Allies wildly
off course,
away to the east,
away from his rallying point,
away from his wife, his son,
his life.
She saw him standing by their fireplace
and it was the last time she saw him.
Nana Q tells me about how
loss has always been a part
of her life...

                     my father's life,
our life,
but that no one ever truly disappears,
no one ever truly goes away.
'He's here,' she says, and points
at her head,
'and here.' She points
at her mouth.
'And here!' Then she points
at her heart.
Nana Q tells me about how
it will stop hurting so much.

The whisper

I think about Mum most days.
I think about the last time I saw her,
not lying in a hospital bed, but
sitting on the sofa
in her dressing gown, readying herself
to say goodbye, and I hadn't realised
till now how hard that must have been,
to say goodbye to her child. I hadn't
realised till now how she must have felt,
knowing I was ill,
sick,
contagious.
And unable to see her,
her unable to see me.
And the whisper in my ear, the one
I couldn't make out before I left
that day, I think she was saying,
'I'll see you soon,'
and that is the grief I will carry with me
for the rest of my life.

Once a week

He goes once a week. I
go too, and Nana Q.
Nana Q and I sit and wait.
Nana Q checks her slips,
and lottery tickets and receipts,
endless bits of paper, her papers.
I sit and wait and think.
I think about how lucky I am.
How lucky we are, to be here
right now, to be in this place
together.
To be here…
                    for each other.
Once a week we all come here, and Dad
goes into the room by himself, on his own.
And we wait; it's all we can do…
sit and wait.
And every week we come here
and the sitting and the waiting
gets easier.

He'll never be complete again

Dad will never be complete again.
He's not an entire person...
not any more.
But what is left
is getting stronger.
What's left
is OK...
is here
with us.
With me.

I begin

It's Monday morning and
we have English lit.
Mr Moore's eyes dart from one
side of the room to
the other.
'Who would like to read the first chapter?'
he says as his pallid eyes fall on me.
I nod. I'm ready,
and we all open our books
at the beginning
and I begin.

For a moment Day 307

For a moment I forgot
about Mum,
Dad...
Nana Q...
For a moment I forgot
about Freya...
I forgot about being ill.
Just for a moment, it was
like it all never happened.
Just for a moment I was
someone else,
I was somewhere else.
And for a moment
I didn't know who I was.
Then it all came back.
Mum...
... Dad
... Nana Q
and Freya
and I felt such a relief
to know everything I know,
because for a moment
I wasn't me
and I wouldn't be me
without all these people.
I wouldn't be me.

A day is a day is a day on repeat Day 311

A day is a day is a day,
each rolls into the next.
The sky is overcast, the
atmosphere is muggy, heavy.
In the school playground
I can see my friends,
looking out for me, and smiling
when they see me.
A day is a day is a day,
each rolls into the next.
The same sounds,
but now they are different,
they feel new.
A day is a day is
a
day.

Daisy

It's 2.40 when I spot
Daisy at the bus stop.
She's on her own
so I sit down next to her
and I talk.
We talk.
We talk for ages.
We miss two buses.
We exchange phone numbers
and we laugh.
We make plans
to talk again,
to meet again,
to smile at each other
again.

Mix-tape on repeat Day 322

I lie on my bed, listening
to music, to a mix-tape I'm making
for me...
for Freya.
Music to help her smile,
music to help keep our minds afloat
on a sea of thoughts,
songs that remind us
of things from before,
things of now and
things yet to come.
Songs to say thank you,
thank you for helping,
helping me to talk,
to open up and meet new people.
And songs to inspire,
songs that act as a time machine
to take us back to
a place and a time:
our place,
our time,
Freya and me.
And I'll be leaving lights on
around the house
as a beacon.

Something new Day 326

Tonight Dad is cooking.
He is trying something new,
a lemon chicken stir-fry
          … with rice noodles.
Nana Q doesn't think she'll
like it.
After, we're going to go for a walk
along the beach and
I'm excited.
We're together
for the first time
in a long time.

Acknowledgements

I know that this book would not have been published without some wonderful and supportive people: my agent, the amazing Becky Bagnell, whose encouragement, dedication and being a constant sounding board have led to this becoming such a special project for me.

Everyone at Unbound, who have shown incredible faith in me and this story, especially the editorial team that have worked with me on this book, DeAndra Lupu and Roisin Heycock, for your insightful, tender suggestions and empathy. Katy Guest, thank you for taking a punt on this project in the first place.

I'm eternally grateful to editor Stephanie King for her work with me on the first drafts of this book: you made this story so much stronger and real, and you will always be a big part of what it has become.

Gemma Southerden and Lindsay Moakes for taking the time to read this before anyone else and for the kind feedback.

To friends and family who have offered kind words and encouraged me along the way with this project, your support means more than you know: Suzanne and Justin, Clare and Steve, James Gadd, David and Suzi Shattock, Tom and Lisa Stallard, Patrick and Sara Toe, Fraser and Sally Williams, Vicky and Matt Mather, Beth and James Proctor, Amy Herbert, Amy Sibley-Allan, Sophie Green, Susie Dent, Rachel Parris, Lisa Francesca Nand, Pauline Barnett, Julie Pettitt, Sue and Megan Terry, Nicole and Team Chatty Hatter, Jim Daly for Team BLANK, Rachel Shenton, Isy Suttie, Cressida Cowell.

A special thanks to Emma Dolan, whose incredible generosity brought me to tears.

To my entire Twitter family, this book wouldn't have happened without you, so huge love and thanks.

To my brother Andy Carpenter, thanks for reminding me about the 'Mint Salad'. Lots of love.

I'm so grateful to my wife Michelle and my two boys Eli and Sonny, who have shown me more love and support than anyone ever could, for being there and listening to me and for giving me the time and space to complete this book. I couldn't do it without you.

A note on the author

Giles Paley-Phillips was born in East Sussex in 1977 and grew up on the south coast. He is the author of nine children's books, including *The Fearsome Beastie* (Maverick Arts Publishing), which won the People's Book Prize 2012 and the Heart of Hawick Children's Book Award 2013, and was Highly Commended in the Forward National Literature Award in the US. It was also shortlisted for the Rotherham Children's Awards 2012. His book *Little Bell and the Moon* (Fat Fox) was shortlisted for the People's Book Prize 2016 and longlisted for the North Somerset Children's Book Award 2017. *One Hundred and Fifty-Two Days*, a semi-autobiographical novel, is his first book for adults.

Giles has appeared on *Good Morning Britain* and an author special of BBC2's *Eggheads*, and is a judge on ITV's *Share a Story*. He also writes a regular book column for *Title* magazine and *Aquila* magazine, and is the producer and co-host of the British Podcast Awards-nominated and iTunes Top 10 podcast *BLANK* with Jim Daly.

Giles still lives in Seaford, East Sussex, with his wife, Michelle, and their two sons, Elijah and Sonny. He is a patron for Action Aid UK.

@eliistender10

Credits

The reference to a private island is from the 1960 Alfred Hitchcock film *Psycho*, written by Joseph Stefano from the novel by Robert Bloch, starring Janet Leigh and Anthony Perkins. It takes place during a conversation between Marion Crane and Norman Bates.

NORMAN BATES: The rain didn't last long, did it? So... where are you off to?

[*Marion looks uncomfortable*]

NORMAN BATES: Sorry. I didn't mean to pry.

MARION CRANE: Oh, I don't know. I guess I'm looking for a private island someplace where I can be alone and no one can find me.

NORMAN BATES: What are you running away from?

MARION CRANE: Why do you ask that?

NORMAN BATES: No reason. No one really runs away from anything. It's like a private trap that holds us in like a prison. You know what I think? I think that we're all in our private traps, clamped in them, and none of us can ever get out. We scratch and we claw, but only at the air, only at each other, and for all of it, we never budge an inch.

Unbound is the world's first crowdfunding publisher, established in 2011.

We believe that wonderful things can happen when you clear a path for people who share a passion. That's why we've built a platform that brings together readers and authors to crowdfund books they believe in – and give fresh ideas that don't fit the traditional mould the chance they deserve.

This book is in your hands because readers made it possible. Everyone who pledged their support is listed below. Join them by visiting unbound.com and supporting a book today.

Lisa Bryan
Murray Buchanan
Mandy Buck
Nicola Buckland
Frances Buckley
Helen Buckley-Hoffmann
Angela Bulkeley
Paulette Burgess
Rebecca Burke
Lindy Burleigh
Ian Burns
Lynda Burns-Hussein
Ann Burrin
Jason Busby
Tanvir Bush
Nick Bushrod
Steven Buss
Marcus Butcher
Darren Butler
Jemma Byres
Angela Byrne
Victoria Byron
Mel C
D. C.
Diane C.O.
Eva Caletkova
Suzanne Callander
Veronica Calleja
TR Cameron
Michelle Campbell
Siân Canning
Alison Cannon
Jo Cannon
Ellie Carley
Sue Carmichael
Lee Carnell
Andy Carpenter
Geraldine Carr
Alison Carter
Anne Carter
Michael Carty
Emma Jo Cash
Zareen Cave
Janina Cebertowicz
Michele Cenzer
Angela Chalkley
Ronke Chalmers
Emma Champion
Marianna Charalambous
Fran Childs
Sue Christensen
Joanne Churcher
Manya Chylinski
Julia Clark
Charlotte Clarke
James Clarke
Louise Clarke
Aimée Clay

Dee Cleary
Ali Cliffe
Sharon Clifton
Will Cohu
Jeremy Coker
Peter Coleman
Ronali Collings
Grace Collins
Louise Collins
Trina Collins
James Conlon
lisa Connaughton-Quinn
Mary Constantinou
Edward Cook
Joanna Cook
Jade Cooper
Karen Cooper
Ruth Cooper-Dickson
Caroline Copeland
Diane Copland
Rebecca Corry
Fi Coulson
Cressida Cowell
Suzy Cragg
Harriet Craig
Paul Craig
Martin Craske
lynne crawford
Gary Crisp
Andrea Crossett
Julia Croyden
Philip Cunnington
Gary Cushway
Janet Cutts
Carla D
Gaudi Daamen
Juliette Dalitz
Nicola Dalleywater
Patricia Daloni
Joanna Dalton
Bradley Dardis
Jane Darroch Riley
Andrew Davies
Charlotte Davies
Jude Davies
Kim Davies
Corrina Davis
J Davis
Katrina Davis
Helen Dawson
Lisa Day
Rachel Delahaye
Stephen Delaney
Hillary Delaney Hall
Liz Delves
Sandra Denbigh
Susanna Dent
Miss Descried

Steve Devine
Claire Devlin
Shireen Dew
Carla Di Mambro
Kevin Diamond
Ian Dickinson
Mike Dicks
Charlotte Dimond
Diane Dingley
Jo Dodd
Michael Dodd
Emma Dolan
Catherine Donald
Irene Donnelly
Emma Donovan
El Dorado
Martin Dowds
Tiffany Dowling
Rory Downey
Emma Downie
Ian Draycott
Morag Drummond
Gillian Duce
Karen Duff
Alison Duncan
Chris Duncan-Scott
Susie Dunham
Andrew Dunkley
Fiona Dunsmore
Karl Durston
Lisa E
Nicola Edward-Rawlings
Greg Edwards
Jean Edwards
Louise Edwards
Rachael Edwards
Sinéad Elizabeth
Dawn Elizabeth Rodriguez
Moira Elliot
Alison Ellis
Janet Ellis
Kirsty Elson
Luke Emmett
Charlotte Ennor
Faye Espley
Anne Eun Mee Tørisen
Ondine Evans
Vivian Evans
Lydia Eve Hughes
Graham Ewens
Alane Farmer
Laura Farrant
Claire Farrow
Dwayne Farver
Anne Marie Fay
Julia Fell
Michelle Feltham
Marie Ferguson

Benne Ferrell
Delila L Fewstin
Bobby Fida
Annabel Finley-Kensett
Val Finnegan
Samantha Fishburn
Tisdale Flannery
Tony Flavin
Geri Fletcher
Adam Flinter
Ricardo Flores
    @EngelAnael
Hayley Foreman
Doug Fort
Fiona Fotheringham
Kerry Fowler
Diane Fowles
Carolyn Fox
Paul Francis
Richard Francis
Victoria Francis
Chris Fraser
Danielle Fraser
Dawn French
Gillian Frew
Julie Fulea
Peter Fullagar
Angela Fuller
Trish Fuller
Kathryn Fullwood
Sinead Fursden
Christina Gabbitas
Suzanne Gagnon
Jenny Gaitskell
Louise Galczynski
Becky Gale
Lindsay Galvin
Jennifer Gandy
Alison Garner
Ruth Garvie
John Gavigan
Selasi Gbormittah
Meloney Geoghegan
Karen Geraghty
Soma Ghosh
Paul-Robert Gibbs
Claire Gibney
Kate Gieler
Suzi Gifford
Richard Gillin
Lilly Girard
Tracy Given
Hattie Gladwell
Claire Glover
Jennie Godfrey
Karla Gonzalez
Suzanne Goss
Elaine Gould

John Graham
Tracey Graham
A grateful reader
Marc Graveney
Gail Gray
Joanne Gray
Nicky Gray
Andrea Greathead
Duncan Green
Sophie Green
William Green
Matthew Greener
Carla Greensmith
Helen Gregory
Donna Gregson
Anne Griffiths
Sara Griffiths
Shay Griffiths
Caroline Guest
Ilise Gunder
Di Gunn
Olga Gutovska
@gypsyhairpoetry
Kip Hakes
Lola Hale
Andy Hall
June Hall
Nicky Hallam
Lynne Hamilton
Celynen Hamlin
Tracy Hammond
Rachel Hanby
Zahra Hankir
David Hannah
Katie Hannant
Alison Hardy
Sean Harkin
Judy Harman
Tina Harman
beverleyJane harper
Sandra Harper
Sian Harries
Rebecca Harris
Sarah Harris
Fran Harrison
Caryl Hart
Susanne Hart
Emma Hartley
Sara Hartshorn
Abbie Hartwell
Ben A Harvey
Mel Haughton
Latoia Haynes
Adam Heaton
Annika Hedly
Rachael Heenan
Lisa Heeps
Susi Hemsley

Robyn Henriegel
Shirlene Hercock
Claire Heron
Claire Heron
Lanah Hewson
Natalie Hibberd
deborah hickey
Gemma Higgins
Sharon Higgs
Paul Higham
Ettaline Hill
Jules Hill
Julie Hill
Patrick Hill
Tim Hillier-Brook
Tara Hilson
Sian Hingston
Ann Hirst
Richelle Hirst
Alison Hobson
Caroline Hodges
Andrea Hodgkinson
Guy Hodgkiss
Melissa Hoffmeyer
Catherine Hokin
John Holborow
The Rabbit Hole
Kat Hollands
Diana Hollins
Dominic Holmes
Jon Holmes
Ali Hope
Suzanne Hope
Maria Hopwood
Alison Horan
Peter Horning
Linda Hotham
Tracy Howells
Kaz Howland
Susan Huck
Vivi Hudson
Liz Hudston
Charlie Hugh-Jones
Grace Hughes
Mary Hulford
Jacqueline Hume
Ruth Hurdon
David Hurst
Sophia Hurst
Jonathan Husband
Nighat Hussain
Donna Hutchinson
Sue Hutchinson
Martin Hywood
Deborah Idle
Amanda Impey
Alan Inglis
Crispinsongs J

Angela Jackson
Ingrid Jackson
Susi Jacobs
Gary James
Kirsteen James
Beverley Jandziol
Jill Janes
Marie Jeff
Marc Jenkins
Alison Jenkins-Wood
Michael Jennings
Rachael Jess
Cathy Johnson
Claire Johnson
Rebecca Johnson
Sarah Johnson
Alan Jones
Anna Jones
Mary Jones
Masato Jones
Nigel Howard Jones
Susanne K
Saskia Kalb
Sara Käll
Catherine Kane
Bridget Kaneen
Areti Karampasi
♥Kate & George… by the sea♥
Katie – Living Life Our Way
Hannah Katsman
Dolores Keaveney
James Keenan
Veronica Kelly
Beatrice Kemp
Ella Kenion
Anna Kennedy
Carol Kennedy
Steve Keohane
Andy Kerr
Robbie Kerry
Lynne Kevill
Naveed Khan
Dan Kieran
Caroline Killelea
Patrick Kincaid
Petra Kindler
Catherine King
Darren King
Stephanie King
Jackie Kirkham
Heleen Kist
Tal M. Klein
Aurora Knight
Caroline Knight
Roohi Kohli
Yuko Komoto
Sophie Koranteng

Richard Kramer
Marie Kreft
Luke Kuhns
Isabel L.
Jeffrey K Laatsch
@LadyEleanirA
LadyEleanorA
Karen Laing
Aline Landrin
Anthony Landsborough
Hannah Langford
Louise Langton-Lockton
John Latham
June Laurenson
Steven Lawley
Dawn Lawrence
Gregory Lawrence
Karen Lawrence
Julie Lawson
Jimmy Leach
Sue Leam
Stephen Leatherdale
Sharon Leavy
Courtney LeCount
Helen Lederer
Nikki Ledingham
Michaela Ledsham
Thomas Leeds
Derek Leitch
Pam Leonard
Leslie
Louise LeVell
Valerie Ley
Rhiannon Limburn
Charmalaine Limson
linda linehan
Gary Lineker
Stephen Little
Jonathan Lodge
Norma Loft
Courtney Long
Veronique Lootens
Katherine Lord-Green
Karen Loughrey
Alex Lovell
Kate Lynch
Anna M
Katrin Maack
Donald MacCuish
Claire Macdonald
Joyce Macdonald
Marie Macfarlane
Stuart Macgarvie
Mandy Machray
Hilary MacMeekin
Joanne Maddison
Lisa Magill
Richard Maguire

Brigid Mahony
Lis Maimaris
Susan Mains
Linda Maitland
Cathy Mallon
Michelle Malone
Ruth Mann
Stephen Manos
Clive Mansfield
Zoe Mantel
Rachael Mantle
Elena Marchevska
Karanasou Maria
Irene Marillat
Aislinn Marshall
Rachel Marshall
Angela Martin
Terry Martin
Lydia Maskery
Julie Mather
Vicky Mather
Leena Mathew
Keith Maxwell
Brendan May
Nuala McCabe
Diane McCarthy
Julie McCavigan
Ameena McColville
Marianne McGhee
Annie McGovern
Deborah McGuire
Susan McGuire
Laura Mcilwraith
Anne-Marie McIntyre
Gwen McKeever
Neil McKenna
Keerie McKenzie
Leza Mckenzie
Martina Mckeown (T.A
Jane McKinnon-Johnson
Mark Mclachlan
Joy McLean
Lauren McLeish
Terry McManus
Roseleen McMenemy
Laura McNeill
Vanella Mead
Alec Meadows
Andrew Meadows
Carole Melia
Carina Mendes
Madeline Mersitz Anklowitz
Eric Messex
Trevor Michael
Christopher Michael Hibbert
Emma Middlemiss

Sarah Milburn
Gina Mildren
Nicky Miller
Vicky Miller
Ellie Millington
Marie Mitchell
Alison Mitchener
John Mitchinson
Helle Moeller
Alastair Monk
Ginny Moon
Lorna Moon
Iain Moore
Jayne Moore
Michelle Moore
Sarah Moraghan
Carol Moran
Jayne Moran
Alice More
Gail Morgan
Jacquelyn Morgan
Liz Morris
Robert Morrison
Bethan Mortimer
Simon Moss
Traci Moss
Niki Moules
Philomena Muinzer
Franc and Amy Mulder
Bettina Munde
Dave Murphy
Julie Murton
Victoria Myers
Jo Myles
Vayu Naidu
Ravi Naik
Julia Nairn
Lisa Nand
Carlo Navato
Claire Naylor
Anton Nelson
Denise Nesbitt
Linda NiChualladh
Clare Nitman
Melissa Noonan
Onneke Northcote-Green
Tania O'Donnell
Aoife O'Dwyer
Harry O'Sullivan
Joanna O'Sullivan
Sophia O'Sullivan
Owen O'Kane
Juliette O'Sullivan
Isolde ÓBrolcháin Carmody
Deschu Oldham
Lucy Oldham
Suzanne Olivante
Karen Oliver

Peter Oliver
Shawna Olsen
Damian ONeil
Tracey Orrow
Amanda Osborne
Tamzin Outhwaite
Nina Over
Claire Owen
Viv Oyolu
J. M. P.
Michael Paley
Alison Palmer
Victoria Parker
Paul Parkerson
Lydgia Parratt
Rachel Parris
Beverley Parsons
Hiran Patel
Jane Patel
Mitch Patterson
Carl Pavo
Chris Pearson
Kimberley Pearson
Denise Peart
Julie Peasgood
camila penrayfon
Anna Peska
Wendy Phelps
Tricia Phillips
Maria Philona
Michelle Carmen Picot
Mary Pierce
Jo Pike
Andrew Pilat
Henryk Pilat
Julia Pilat
Lewis Pilat
Jane Pink
Federica Pisanu
Joel Piveteau
Sarah Playforth
MATOULA Ploumidi
Sal Plummer
Clare Pollard
Justin Pollard
David Polus
Aron Pope
Crystal Pope
Seren Portia
Cassie Powney
M Prescott
Amanda Priestley
Beth Procter
Mark Procter
Alexandra Prod'homme
Connie Prokuda
Vicki Psarias-Broadbent
Sarah Ann Pugh

Katie Pullen
Ewen Purcell
Geraldine Purcell
Summer Quigley
Nanci Quinn
Ivanka Radkova
Steven Ramage
Erica Ramsey
Helen Randall
Natalie Randall
Robert Randolph
Charlotte Raveney
Emily Rawlinson
Peter Rayney
Soni Razdan
Nick Redman
Leo Reece
Mark Reed
Sheryl Reed Wells
Helen Reid
Sarah Reid
Susanna Reid
Stephanie Reilly
Kelly Reiterman
Joanna Ren
Sarah Rennie
Catherine Renton
Bryony Rest
Elizabeth Reynolds
Katie Reynolds
Onnica Rheade
Joanna Rhydderch
Joanne Ribinson
Catherine Rice
Amy Rich
Emma Richardson
Linda Ricketts
Eileen Ridge
Mandi Riseman
Karen Ritchie
Bob Robb
Vicki Roberti
Jane Roberts
Lucie Roberts
Bob Robertson
Pam Robins
Lynn Robinson
Suzy Robinson
Arelis Rodriguez-Farradas
Adrienne Rogers
James Rogers
Nicholas Rogers
Antonia Rookley
Debbie Rooney
Ellie Roosinovich
Kate Rose
Ethan Rosenberg
Rebecca Rouillard

Wendy Rowcroft
Siobhan Rowden
Nora Rowland
Vanessa Rowlands
Mary Rudge
Nancy M Ruff
Helen Rule
Sophie Rumble
Deana Russell
Tanweer S Chowdhury MBE
June Sadler
Jules Saich
John Salako
Barbara Salmon
Pauline Salmon
Tim Sands
Gareth Saunders
Sonia Saville
Petra Saxby
Dan Scholes
Antoinette Scivier
Annabel Scott
Ruth Scott-Williams
Emma Scullion
jenn sebastion
Tanja Seck
Lauren Seeley
Scott Seivwright
Helen Seymour
Nicola Shanley
Fari Sharif
Eve Sharman
Rose Sharpe
David Shattock
Ann-Marie Shaw
Amanda Sheard
Joanne Sheldon
Mark Sheldon-Jones
Dorothy Shenton
R Shenton
Claire Sheppard
Diana Sheridan
Gillian Shields
Samantha Shiner
Linda Shoare
Amy Sibley-Allen
Sarah Siggs
Graham Simms
Emily Simpson
Julia Sinclair
Sam Singh
Debbie Slater
Hazel Slattery
David Slattery-Christy
Annie Smith
Don Smith
Helen Smith
Liz Smith

Mal Smith
Michael Smith
Siobhan Smith
Adele Sneddon
Amelia Snelling
Gemma Southerden
Karin Sowden
Ursula Speidel
Debbie Spence
Gabriella Spiniello
John Sprackland
Julie St. John
Adele Stach-Kevitz
Thomas Stallard
Aleksa Stanišić
Paul Statham
Phil Steer
Peter Stefanovic
Iris Stelar
mark stephens
Laura Stevens
Diana Stewart
Louise Stewart
Julie Stonham
Janice Storey
Helen Stow
sarah Strahan
Roar Strand
Charlotte Stranks
Andrew Street
Marla Stromberg (CBT
     Canary Wharf)
Lona Stuart
Heidi Sumner
Sharron Sumner
Nora Surojegin
Sali Sutherland
Isy Suttie
Denise Sutton
Rebecca Swansbury
Chris Sweeney
Laura Sykes
Maureen Symons
Kat Szladicsek
Alastair Tams
Kellie Tapuae
Wanda Tarr
Gail Taylor
Joel Taylor
Sarah Taylor
Susan Taylor
Wonderful Teachers
Sue Terry
Jon the Statistician
Suzie Theobald
Gina Thomas
Penny Thomas
David Thompson

Julia Thompson
Steph Thompson
Graham Thorpe
Jenny Tidman
Lucy Tochel
Patrick Toe
Lesley Toles
Paul Towey
Theresa Travis
Julie Travis-Drew
Kate Trenaman
Zoë Tribello
Amelia Troubridge
Sharon Trudgett
Jennifer Tubbs
Larry Tucker
Jane Turner
Rick Turner
Emily Turnham
Dan Udale
Sophia Ufton
Angela Uglow
Lisa Ummat
Karen Underhill
Patricia Ⓥ
Jake Valenta
Evelyne van Eijck
Julie Vardalia
Tarun Varma
Mike Verwoert
Mary Victoria
Alisa Vieora
Tushar Vince
Erik von Brunn
Jonathan Wade
Jenny Walker
Martin Walker
Anne-Marie Wallace
Breda Walton
Marcus Ward
Caroline Ward Vine
Liz Ware
Susan Warlow
Cheryl Warner
Emma Washford
Sam Washington
Jane Waterman
Rebecca Waters
Rosie Waters
opheliaofavon11@gmail.com
     Watkins
Kim Watkiss
Joanne Watson
Miranda Watson
Craig Watt
Andy Watts
peteway Way
Jo Weaver

Pauline Weaver
Richard Webb
Trey Webb
Justine Weir
Janette Welford
Katherine Wells
Moira Wesson
Samuel West
Laura Westaway
Suzanne Westhead
Sarah Westwood
Julie Weyer
Tess Wheeler
Bob White
Cheryl White
Kathya Kathya White
Lori Whitlock
Heidrun Wielage

Tess Wigginton
Tien Wilde
Karen Wilkinson
Amanda Willett
Adam William Inglis
Fraser Williams
Hayley Williams
Jane Williams
Sharon Williams
Simon Williams
Anne Willicombe
Donald Wilson
Katherine Wilson
Mak Wilson
Nick Wilson
Penelope Wincer
Kathi Windheim
Stacey Winters

Claire Withers
Nicola Wood
Paul Wood
Lois Woodhead
Sam Wooding
Jacqui Woodward
Kerry Wordsworth
sOOz world
Janice Wynne
Nicola Yerrill
Dyan Yoder
Deborah Youd
DustyCody Young
Susanne Young
Dawn Zilllla
Andrew Zolnai

With special thanks to the following people for their generous
and 'collectably social' support of this book.

Deborah Benavides – @docdeb83
Nicola Buckland – @nicclesb
Ann Burrin
Jo Cannon – @joannacannon
Ronali Collings – @RonaliCollings
Greg Edwards – @rednbluegreg
Ondine Evans
Tony Flavin – @deaconTF
Adam Flinter – @adamflinter
Ricardo Flores – @EngelAnael
Christina Gabbitas – @christigabbitas
Ilise Gunder – @girlybones1978
Latoia Haynes – @toiagoia
Robyn Henriegel – @Schuting
Adam William Inglis – @AWInglis
Ingrid Jackson – @RadLibitum
Rebecca Johnson – @oldboldmouldy
Anthony Landsborough – @AELandsborough
Thomas Leeds
Clive Mansfield – @MansfieldClive
Terry McManus – @tmcwildart
Peter Oliver – @PeterGOliver_RT
Anna Peska – @anna_p__
Steven Ramage – @steven_ramage
Helen Randall – @helenrandall110
Scott Seivwright
Linda Shoare – @lindashoare
Phil Steer – @philsteer64
Roar Strand – @roarstr & @roarstrand
Marla Stromberg (CBT Canary Wharf) – @MarlaStromberg
Joel Taylor – @JoelTaylorhack
Theresa Travis – @s9tmt
Martin Walker – @MNW533
Miranda Watson – @mirminx